W9-CKT-157

⁊ BETSY & GIULIO MAESTRO ⁊

Exploration AND Conquest

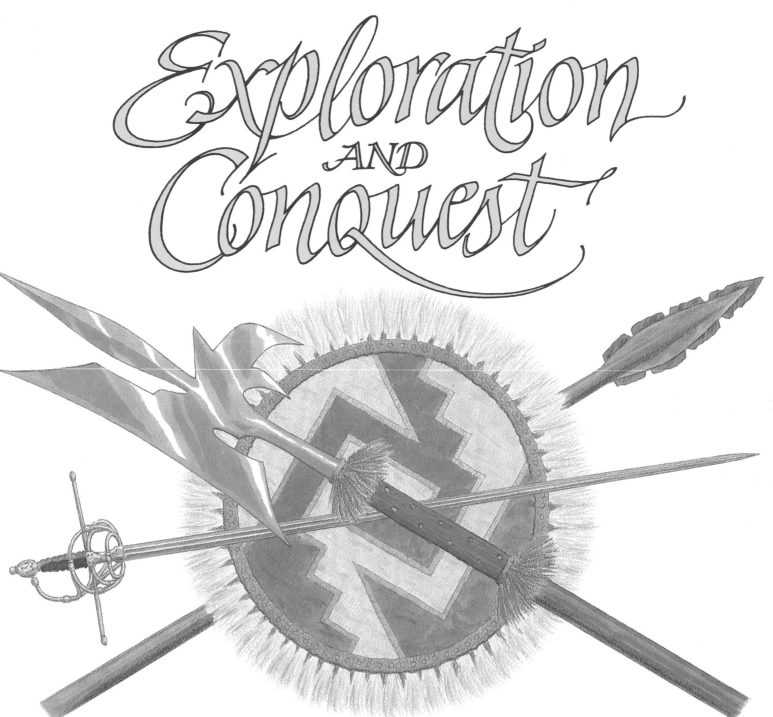

THE AMERICAS AFTER COLUMBUS: 1500-1620

A MULBERRY PAPERBACK BOOK · NEW YORK

Jefferson-Madison
Regional Library
Charlottesville, Virginia

WITHDRAWN

1712 1284

Text copyright © 1994 by Betsy C. Maestro
Illustrations copyright © 1994 by Giulio Maestro

All rights reserved. No part of this book may be reproduced or utilized in any form or by
any means, electronic or mechanical, including photocopying, recording, or by any
information storage or retrieval system, without permission in writing from the Publisher.
Inquiries should be addressed to Lothrop, Lee & Shepard Books, a division of William
Morrow & Company, Inc., 1350 Avenue of the Americas, New York, New York 10019.
Printed in the United States of America.

The illustrations in this book were done in watercolor and colored pencil on illustration
board. The display type was hand-lettered by Giulio Maestro.
The text type was set in ITC Garamond Book.

The Library of Congress has cataloged the Lothrop, Lee & Shepard edition of EXPLORATION
AND CONQUEST as follows:
Maestro, Betsy. Exploration and conquest: the Americas after Columbus,
1500–1620, by Betsy and Giulio Maestro.
p. cm.
ISBN 0-688-09267-5.—ISBN 0-688-09268-3 (lib. bdg.)
1. America—Discovery and exploration—Juvenile literature.
2. America—History—To 1810—Juvenile literature. [1. America—Discovery and
exploration. 2. America—History—To 1810.] I. Maestro, Giulio, ill. II. Title. E121.M27
1994 970.01—dc20 93-48618 CIP AC

3 5 7 9 10 8 6 4
First Mulberry Edition, 1997
ISBN 0-688-15474-3

Christopher Columbus was not the first to discover the Americas. But his voyages led to the European exploration of the New World. In 1492, Columbus (Cristoforo Colombo) sailed west across the Atlantic Ocean in search of a sea route to the Far East. European countries had begun to trade with India and China more than a century before, using overland routes that were difficult to travel. Explorers began to search for a faster sea route to the Orient. The Portuguese sailed south around the tip of Africa and across the Indian Ocean.

It was Spain's search for its own sea route that led to the discovery of the New World. When Columbus sighted land, he was sure that he had reached the Orient. However, other explorers soon realized that the lands he had found were new to them—part of a continent they had not known existed. They would have to find a way to sail around this land if they were to reach the Far East.

At the time of Columbus's voyages, Spain and Portugal commanded such powerful fleets of ships that no nation could challenge them at sea. Portugal had trading posts in Africa and would soon reach India by ship. So Spain eagerly looked west to establish new trading posts and its own sea route to the Far East. In 1494, the two nations signed an important agreement dividing the "unclaimed" parts of the world between them. Portugal was given control of the African sea route and the Indian Ocean to the east, and Spain the right to explore and trade in the Americas to the west. Only the area that is now Brazil came under Portuguese control.

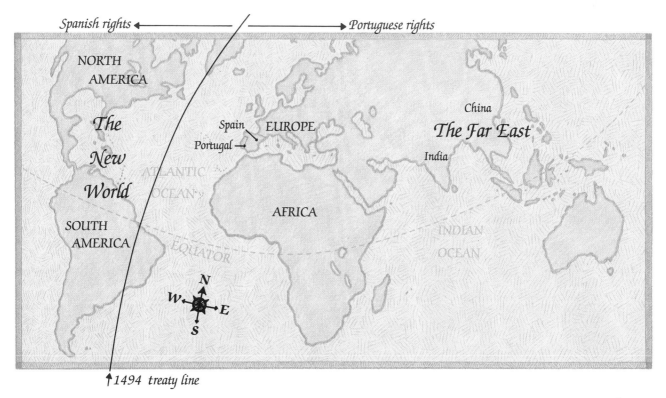

Spanish rights ← _____ → Portuguese rights

NORTH AMERICA

The New World

SOUTH AMERICA

EUROPE
Spain
Portugal →

AFRICA

EQUATOR

China
The Far East
India

INDIAN OCEAN

ATLANTIC OCEAN

N
W · E
S

↑ 1494 treaty line

Spanish explorers soon discovered that the New World was full of people who called it their home. People had been living in the Americas for thousands of years before Columbus arrived. But the Spanish gave little thought to these inhabitants who had already explored and claimed the land for themselves. The Spanish considered the natives heathens, or nonbelievers, because they did not worship the Christian God. The Spanish did not respect the native religions or the rights of these people, whom they thought of as uncivilized savages—barely human. They felt perfectly free to take their land, their riches, and often their lives. During the years of the European search for a passage west, the lives of the inhabitants of the islands and continents of the New World would be changed forever.

As the Spanish searched for a westward passage, they also looked for goods and riches to send back to Spain. Explorers like Vasco Núñez de Balboa began to venture farther inland. In 1513, he made his way through the dense jungles of Panama and sighted the Pacific Ocean. That same year, Juan Ponce de León explored some of what is now Florida. Six years later, Ferdinand Magellan (Fernando de Magalhães) set out on what would become the first known voyage around the world. New maps gave Europeans some idea of the true size of the earth.

While they were exploring areas of what is now Mexico, the Spaniards heard thrilling stories of huge cities filled with gold. The thought of such fabulous wealth was irresistible to them, and they turned from their search for a passage to a search for gold—from exploration to conquest. Large expeditions of soldiers, called conquistadores, were sent out to claim land and riches for the king and the Church of Spain. With them went priests who tried to force the native people to accept the Catholic faith. However, these people had their own strong beliefs and often had no idea what the Spanish were trying to teach them. They resisted the Spaniards' attempts to change their way of life.

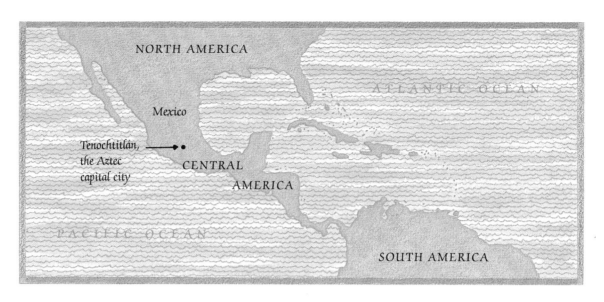

In 1519, Hernán Cortés and hundreds of armed soldiers arrived to try to take Mexico from the Aztecs. The Aztecs were a powerful people with thousands of soldiers. Although the Spaniards were greatly outnumbered, they had swords and firearms, crossbows and cannons, and horses, which were new and frightening to Native Americans. The Spanish soldiers also received some unexpected help from neighboring enemies of the Aztecs.

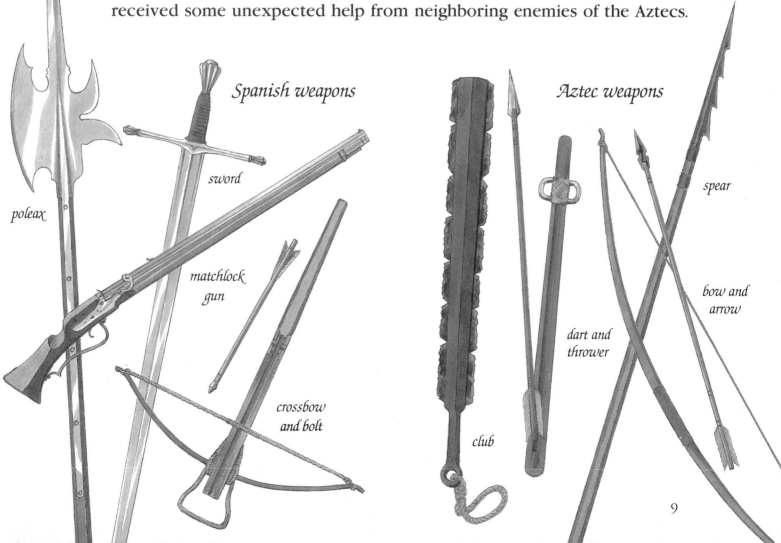

Spanish weapons

poleax

sword

matchlock gun

crossbow and bolt

Aztec weapons

spear

bow and arrow

dart and thrower

club

Pretending to come in friendship, Cortés and his army entered the city of Tenochtitlán as guests of the Aztec emperor, Motecuhzoma Xocoyotzin, whom the Spanish called Montezuma. The Spaniards were amazed and impressed by the size and splendor of the Aztec capital. The people dressed in great finery with ornaments of feathers, gold, and jewels, and Cortés and his men were given rooms in a beautiful palace. Later, when the emperor visited there, the Spanish took him prisoner. They were "guests" of the Aztecs, but were so outnumbered that they were forced to stay for months. Cortés was allowed to leave Tenochtitlán for a short while, and in his absence, the Spanish soldiers launched an attack on unarmed Aztecs. The whole city rose up in revolt. When Cortés returned, the Aztecs forced him into a retreat, during which thousands of Spanish soldiers were killed.

Thousands of Aztecs, including Montezuma, were also killed in the battle. Many more died of smallpox and other diseases brought by the Spaniards. Although the Aztecs drove the invaders from their city, the empire was greatly weakened and their victory was short-lived. In less than a year, Cortés returned to Tenochtitlán with an army of Spanish and native Tlaxcalan soldiers. In a battle that lasted for seventy-five days, the conquistadores destroyed the city and brought down the Aztec Empire. By the middle of 1521, after three years of fighting, the Spanish controlled all of Mexico.

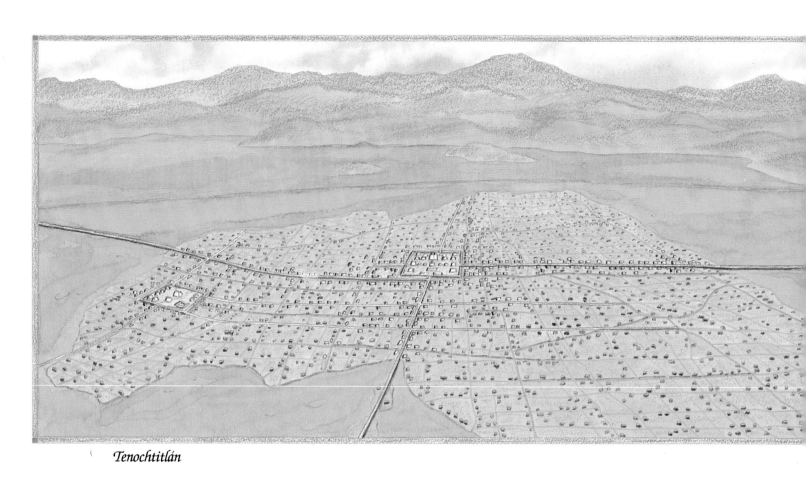

Tenochtitlán

The temples of Tenochtitlán

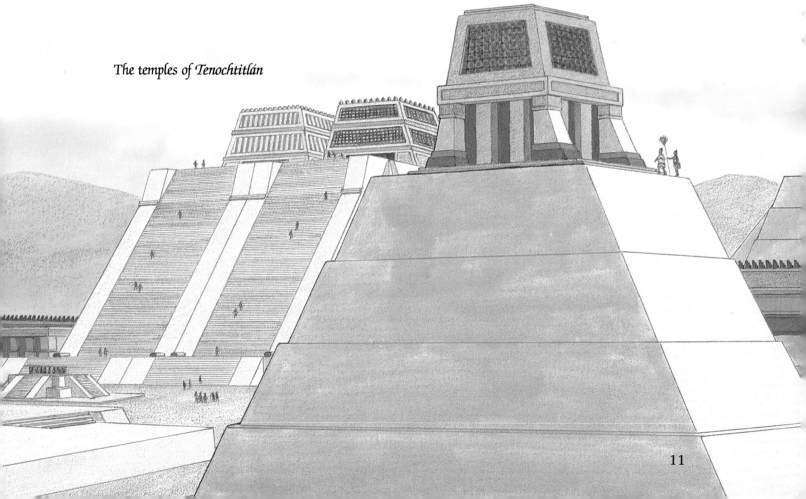

The Inca road system

Caxamarca

PERU

Cuzco, the Inca capital city

SOUTH AMERICA

The Inca Empire

Francisco Pizarro, another Spanish conquistador, heard tales of fantastic riches to be found high in the Andes Mountains of Peru, in the land of the Inca. Their empire was the largest in South America, stretching for nearly three thousand miles from north to south. Pizarro began his quest to reach the Inca Empire in 1524, but failed. Seven years later, with Hernando de Soto and an army of a few hundred men, Pizarro set out again. The Spaniards traveled along the excellent system of Inca roads and bridges on their long, exhausting journey.

In 1532, when Pizarro and de Soto finally arrived at Caxamarca, where the Inca leader Atahualpa was staying, the emperor was expecting them. Inca soldiers and messengers had been watching the progress of the Spaniards throughout their journey. Atahualpa, confident of his power and safety, invited the bearded strangers to meet with him. When Pizarro and the others came down into the valley, they were stunned at the sight of Atahualpa's vast army. The Spaniards retreated and set up camp in the protected area of the town square, where they invited the emperor to visit them the next day.

The Spaniards waited all day until finally, at sunset, Atahualpa arrived with thousands of unarmed soldiers and attendants. The square was empty except for a Spanish priest, who asked the emperor to accept the Christian faith. When the Inca leader refused, the Spaniards launched a surprise attack, emerging from the buildings where they had been hiding. They killed most of the Incas and captured Atahualpa, holding him for ransom. Even though a huge payment was made—thousands of pounds of gold and silver—the Spaniards executed the emperor. The Inca Empire, already greatly weakened by civil war and disease, soon fell to the Spanish.

Immense quantities of gold and silver, once the property of the Aztecs and Incas, were shipped to Spain to fill the king's treasury. Spain became the richest and most powerful seafaring nation on earth.

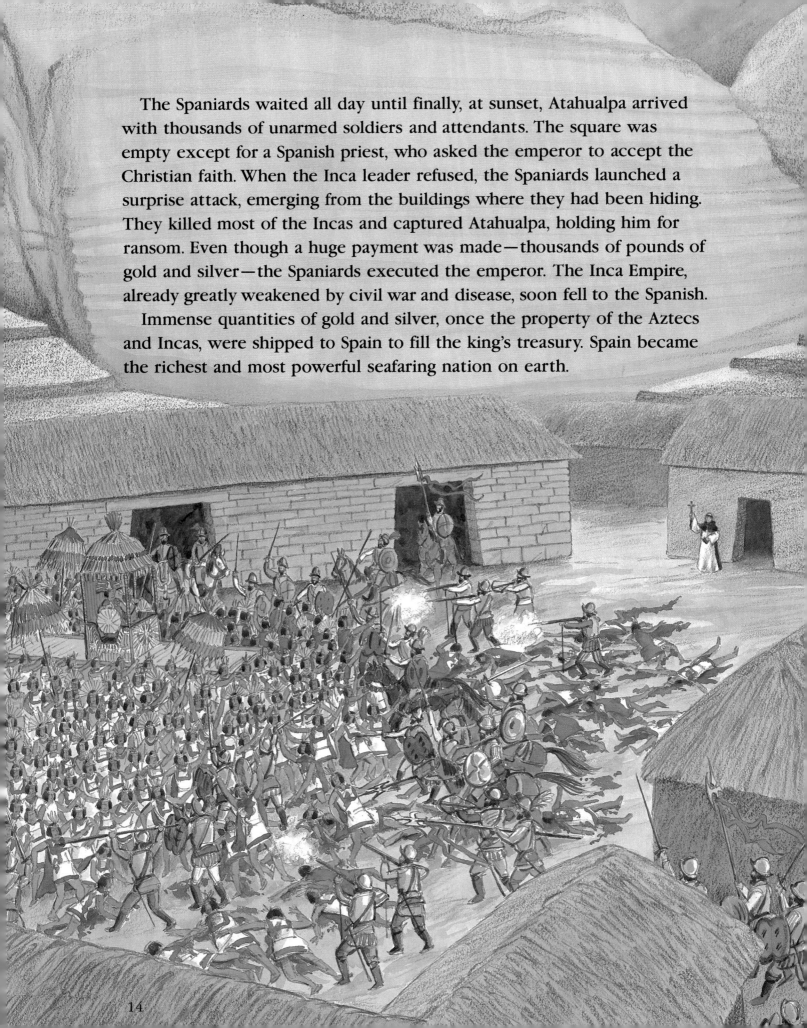

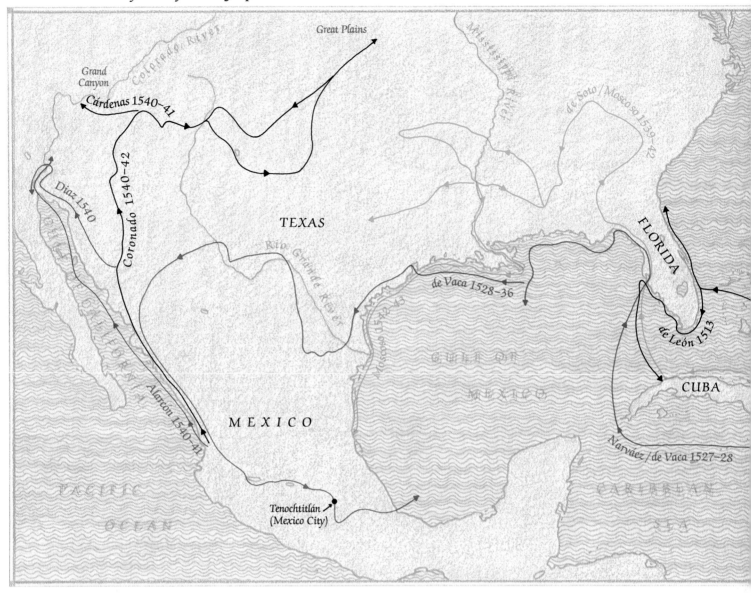

While Pizarro was in Peru, other Spanish explorations were under way farther north. Alvar Núñez Cabeza de Vaca, with three other survivors of an earlier failed expedition, spent about six years living among native tribes in what is now Texas. Although separated from each other, they stayed alive by trading their labor and skills for food and shelter. When they were reunited, they wandered westward before turning south to Mexico. On the way, they heard stories of great buffalo herds and of the massive pueblo cities of the Hopi and Zuni peoples. When Cabeza de Vaca and his companions reached Mexico City in 1536, their adventures inspired other explorers to head north.

After helping Pizarro in Peru, Hernando de Soto was eager to stake his own claim to territory and fortune. He arrived in Florida in 1539 to search for gold with more than six hundred conquistadores. As they traveled throughout the southeast, they brought misery to the tribes they encountered, including the Choctaw, Creek, and Chickasaw. De Soto and his men burned villages, stole food, and killed or captured thousands of people. The natives, at first friendly, became hostile to the intruders, causing trouble for them whenever and however they could. During the long expedition—three thousand miles in four years—half the Spaniards died of starvation or disease. De Soto himself perished and was buried in the sands of the Mississippi River in 1542. About three hundred men made it back to Mexico—without their leader and without the gold for which they longed.

Other Spaniards were also searching for treasure. Francisco Vásquez de Coronado left Mexico in 1540, with hundreds of soldiers and native guides, to search for the fabled Seven Cities of Gold. No one knew whether this land of great wealth really existed, but the desire for riches was so strong that no journey seemed too long to attempt. In two years, this expedition covered thousands of miles, reaching the Great Plains and the Colorado River and Grand Canyon. But these places held no interest for Coronado and his men; they had come only to find gold. Having failed, they returned to Mexico, bitter and defeated.

After the fabulous wealth discovered in Mexico and Peru, the North American expeditions were a tremendous disappointment, and the Spanish gave up the quest for gold there. They did, however, establish permanent settlements in Florida and in the southwest of what is now the United States. They built schools, churches, and missions and brought their own rich cultural heritage to the Americas. In places where Spanish culture flourished, native cultures were forced to adopt the Spanish way of life or flee to other, as yet undisturbed, areas.

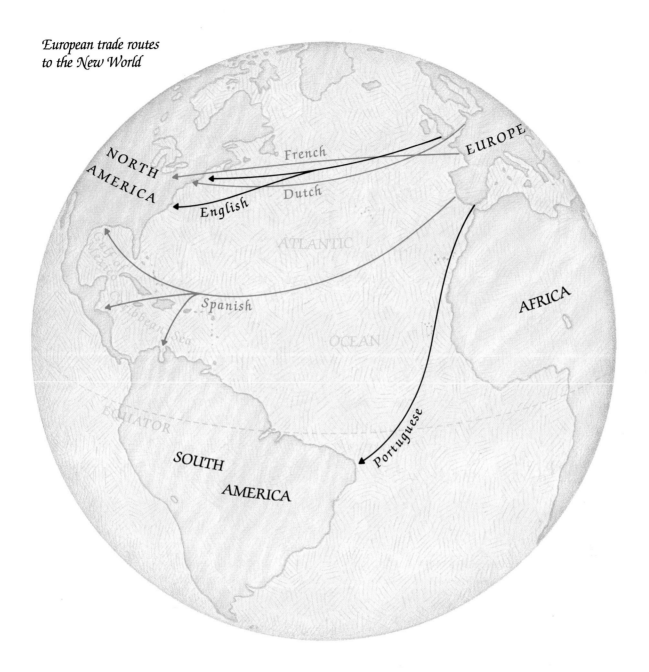

England, France, and Holland were also interested in the New World. They too wanted to find trade routes to the Far East and establish trading posts in the Americas. Yet none of these nations dared to openly challenge the Spanish at sea. They couldn't sail into the waters of the Caribbean Sea and the Gulf of Mexico, known as the Spanish Main. Spanish America, to the south, was completely closed to them. Once Spain lost interest in most of North America, other European countries felt free to explore there and to claim land for themselves.

Early maps of the western hemisphere showed Japan and China
very close to the west coast of North America.

Many European explorers believed that there was a northern sea route — a passage through North America — to the Orient. Since John Cabot (Giovanni Caboto) made his first voyage for England in 1497, there had been great interest in the idea of this northwest passage. Once Portugal and Spain had routes to the Far East, other nations were anxious to locate a passage in the north for themselves.

After Cabot's voyages, both France and Portugal sent fishing fleets into North American waters. The Portuguese founded a small fishing village on Cape Breton Island, Nova Scotia, in about 1522. Despite the harsh climate, the plentiful fish offered great reward.

In 1524, the French sent Giovanni da Verrazano, an experienced Italian seaman, to explore the North American coastline. Near North Carolina, Verrazano sighted what he thought was a large inland sea, a possible beginning to a passageway. This "Oriental Sea" was probably Pamlico Sound and was not a sea at all. Along the route, crew members were often sent ashore to trade, and sometimes small boats filled with friendly native people would come out to meet the ship. These mainly peaceful encounters seem to have been the first contacts between Europeans and these groups of Native Americans. Unfortunately, Verrazano and other explorers often captured some of these people to take back to Europe as curiosities.

Giovanni da Verrazano

From the Carolinas to Maine, Verrazano noted every detail of the trip. He wrote of good harbors and fertile farmland, of fresh lakes and streams. He gave detailed colorful descriptions of the people he called "Indians," finding most of them approachable and helpful. Verrazano and his crew were the first Europeans to view the Hudson River, New York Bay, and Cape Cod. The French kept all of this useful information to themselves, as they did not want other countries to profit from Verrazano's voyage. Word of his "Oriental Sea" somehow leaked out, though, and for many years other explorers searched vainly for this nonexistent passage to the Orient.

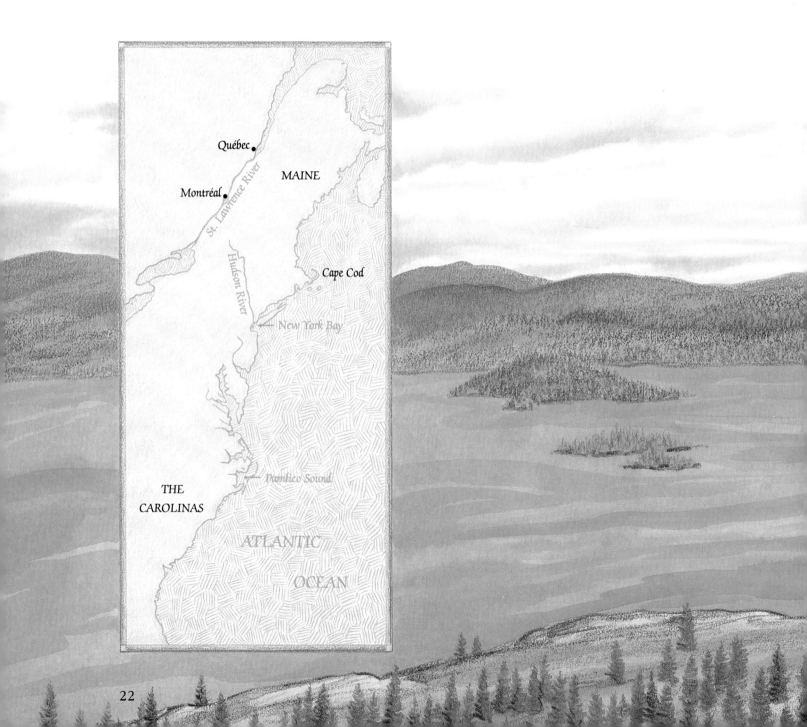

In 1534, France sent Jacques Cartier on the first of three voyages to search for a northwest passage in what is now Canada. With the help of native guides, he was able to reach the sites where Québec and Montréal now stand. Cartier and his party traded ideas and information as well as goods and supplies with the Hurons, Micmac, and other native peoples. Although Cartier explored a thousand miles into the interior and claimed new territory for France, he discovered no passage and found no gold or jewels. Disappointed, the French gave up their efforts in North America for sixty years. Over time, the real riches of the north—lumber, furs, and fish—would prove to have greater value than the gold and silver of the south.

By about 1560, England, France, and Holland all had large sailing fleets and wanted to be able to trade freely around the world. But trading was still limited by Spanish and Portuguese control of sea routes and important ports. At first, these countries tried to coexist peacefully at sea with the Spanish and Portuguese, but they were challenged at every turn. They were afraid that open defiance would lead to war. So they began to defy Spain secretly—by smuggling goods into the smaller ports, avoiding Spanish ships and authorities.

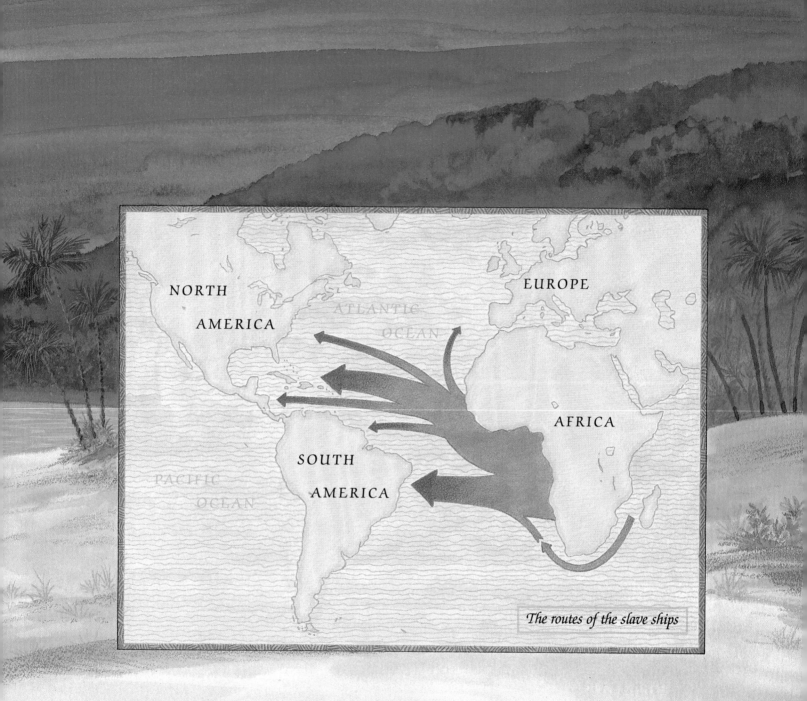

The routes of the slave ships

John Hawkins was one of the English captains most active in smuggling goods into Spanish ports. Plantation owners along the coast of South America were eager to deal with him for the supplies they wanted. Thousands of laborers were needed to run the plantations. At first, the owners had used Native Americans as slaves, but these workers soon died of starvation and disease. Hawkins and other European merchant captains found a way to provide the slaves for the Spanish plantations. On their way to the New World, they began to stop along the African coast, where they picked up large numbers of unwilling voyagers.

The European slave trade began earlier—in the 1400s—when the Portuguese transported African slaves to Portugal and then to Spain. By 1505, African slaves had begun to arrive in the Americas. Portugal, Spain, Holland, and then England became involved in this profitable but miserable business. Merchant captains would spend several months traveling along the African coast, making deals with Portuguese traders or African chieftains. Through armed force and kidnapping, men, women, and children were gathered and chained hand and foot. They were branded like animals and shoved into the stinking holds of ships.

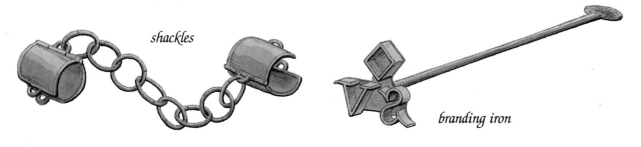

shackles

branding iron

Slaves were often held at forts called barracoons to await the long ocean voyage.

Crowded into these airless places for five to ten weeks, the captives were hardly fed. Almost half of this human cargo would die before reaching the New World. The survivors were sick and weak and frightened. Their futures held nothing but misery. Sadly, slavery was a highly profitable business for the traders. High demand and profits would keep the slave trade alive for hundreds of years. In that time, at least ten million Africans would be brought to the Americas as slaves.

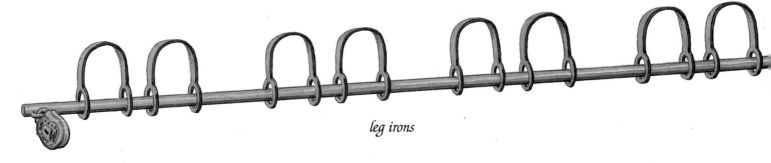

leg irons

John Hawkins

Francis Drake

Around 1560, many seaman-adventurers became actively involved in challenging the Spanish in the New World. Hawkins's cousin Francis Drake was the most famous of these adventurers. Drake hated the Spanish and longed for the day when England could freely sail anywhere in the world. He made six voyages to the Spanish Main over thirty years, using elaborate and incredibly daring plans to raid Spanish ships and ports. Drake's success greatly embarrassed the Spanish, who were forced to give their ships and ports more protection.

Drake's third voyage, 1577–80

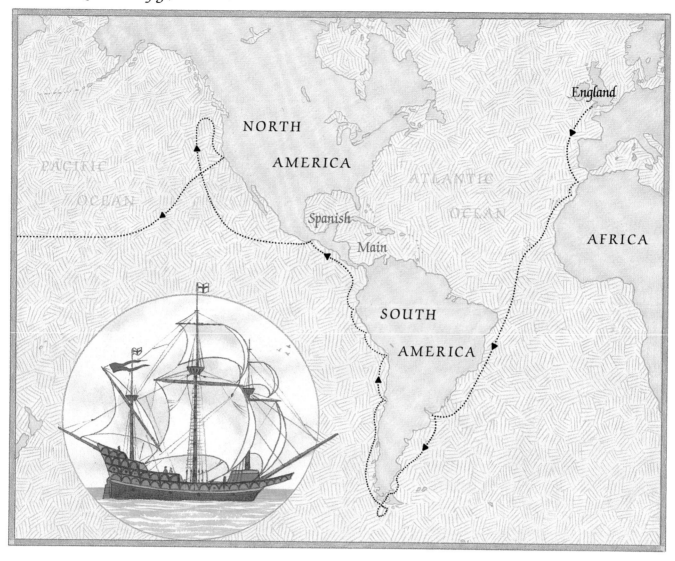

Drake's third voyage, in 1577, was his most difficult and successful. To anger the Spanish and prove that English ships could sail where they pleased, he was determined to follow Magellan's route to the Pacific. Fierce storms and mutinous crews caused four of his ships to be scuttled or sent home. Only the *Golden Hind* sailed out into the Pacific and up the American west coast. Raiding Spanish ships along the way for treasure and supplies, Drake and his crew eventually sailed north to California and possibly to Oregon.

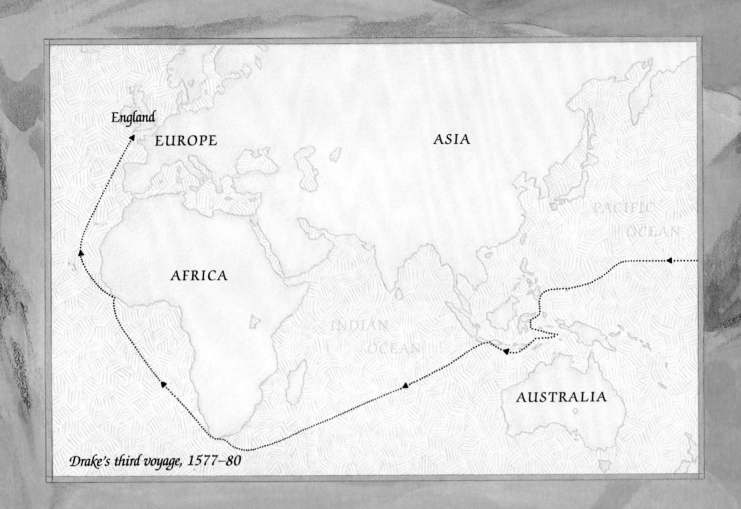

England

EUROPE

ASIA

AFRICA

PACIFIC
OCEAN

INDIAN
OCEAN

AUSTRALIA

Drake's third voyage, 1577–80

Leaving the California coast, Drake followed Magellan's route across the Pacific and Indian oceans, rounding the tip of Africa and then sailing north for home. The *Golden Hind* reached England in September 1580. Drake and his crew had sailed for almost three years and had traveled thirty-four thousand miles. Drake was hailed as a hero and honored by the English queen, Elizabeth I. He had proved that Spain could be challenged for control of the seas. Eight years later, England would defeat the Spanish Armada, the strongest naval fleet on earth, and Spain's absolute power at sea would come to an end.

While Drake was sailing Spanish waters, other Englishmen were continuing the quest for a northwest passage. Beginning in 1576, Martin Frobisher, Humphrey Gilbert, and John Davis all made voyages to North America. They explored the icy regions of what are now Greenland, Labrador, and Baffin Island. Although these explorers didn't discover a passage or find valuable minerals, they did contribute new information for future expeditions. Over time, Europeans came to fully appreciate the value of the natural resources: timber, furs, and fish. Soon they were eager to establish permanent footholds in the Americas — colonies with which they could trade.

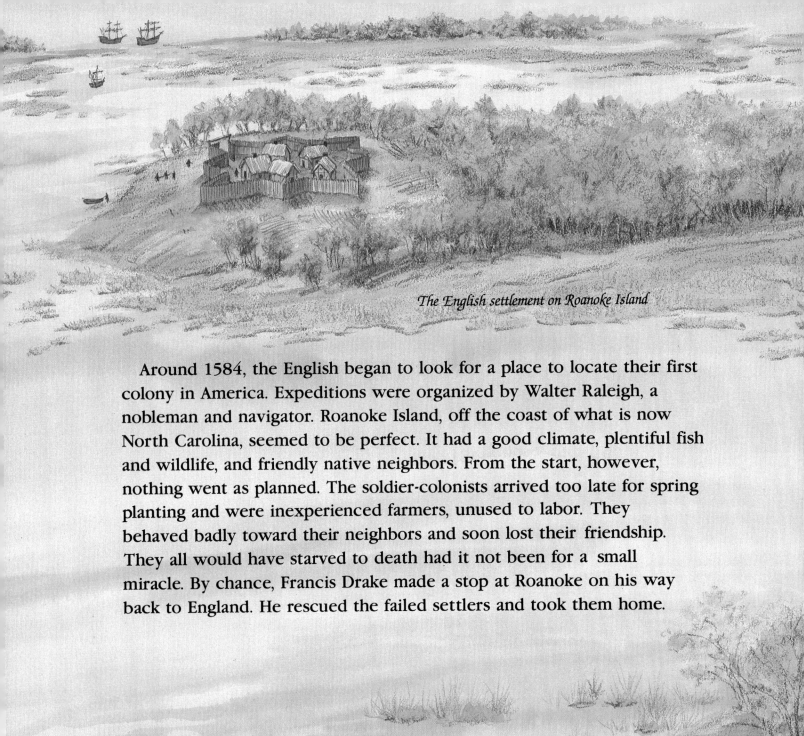

The English settlement on Roanoke Island

Around 1584, the English began to look for a place to locate their first colony in America. Expeditions were organized by Walter Raleigh, a nobleman and navigator. Roanoke Island, off the coast of what is now North Carolina, seemed to be perfect. It had a good climate, plentiful fish and wildlife, and friendly native neighbors. From the start, however, nothing went as planned. The soldier-colonists arrived too late for spring planting and were inexperienced farmers, unused to labor. They behaved badly toward their neighbors and soon lost their friendship. They all would have starved to death had it not been for a small miracle. By chance, Francis Drake made a stop at Roanoke on his way back to England. He rescued the failed settlers and took them home.

A new group of colonists arrived on the island in 1587 with their leader, John White. There were 150 men, women, and children, including many farmers. They rebuilt the settlement and planted crops, and over the summer a child was born. She was White's grandchild, Virginia Dare — the first English baby born in North America. Later, White returned to England for supplies. Because of the fighting with Spain, he could not get back to Roanoke for three long years. On his return, he found the island completely deserted. Despite many searches, no trace of the settlers could be found. To this day, no one knows what became of the Lost Colony.

An Algonquian settlement on the mainland

When he became king in 1603, James I encouraged the formation of large trading companies in order to set up colonies in North America. In 1606, the Virginia Company sent Captain John Smith to America with more than one hundred new settlers. They started a colony, which they named for the king, on what is now the James River in Virginia. The carpenters, craftsmen, gentlemen, and soldiers built a fortress for protection. Unfortunately, their supplies did not last long, and many died of starvation and illness. Kindly natives brought food and saved Jamestown from extinction.

John Smith

Once it was resupplied, the colony thrived under Smith's leadership. By 1609, about five hundred men lived in Jamestown. However, when John Smith returned to England, the colony experienced its worst winter. Food was scarce, disease spread, and relations with nearby tribes had become strained and hostile. Only sixty-five settlers survived what was called the "starving time." In spring, the arrival of fresh supplies gave the colonists new hope. But it was a young man named John Rolfe who truly saved the colony. He began to grow tobacco, a very profitable crop; and he married Pocahontas, a daughter of an important tribal chief. Jamestown entered a period of peace and prosperity.

The Jamestown fort

Around 1619, important events in Jamestown helped to shape the future of English colonial life in North America. Women arrived in the colony, marking the beginning of family life. A Dutch trading ship unloaded twenty African slaves who were put to work in the tobacco plantation—beginning a system of slavery that would last for more than two hundred years. Also about this time, a meeting was held in Jamestown. Representatives from all the small nearby settlements gathered to make up a set of laws for everyone to follow. That was the start of colonial self-government.

Relations with area tribes continued to worsen. Native Americans were tired of making agreements with the white settlers only to have them broken again and again. They did not want to share their land and hunting grounds with greedy people who could not be trusted. Finally, they revolted. Fighting between the Native Americans and the English went on for more than ten years, with many deaths on both sides. In the end, the white settlers forced the native people off their homelands. To preserve their own ways, these tribes moved farther into the interior. Jamestown became the first permanent English colony at great human cost and suffering.

Farther north, in Canada, the French had developed a profitable fur trade and wanted to found a more permanent colony. Samuel de Champlain began to explore these northern woodlands in 1603, following the path of Cartier. He founded the city of Québec and opened a trading post near Montréal. Champlain became the first European to explore the Ottawa River, Lake Ontario and Lake Huron, and what is now upper New York State. He was able to make these difficult journeys into unknown wilderness only with the help of friendly Ottawas, Hurons, and other natives willing to act as guides and interpreters. Champlain spent more than thirty years in his adopted homeland of Canada.

Samuel de Champlain

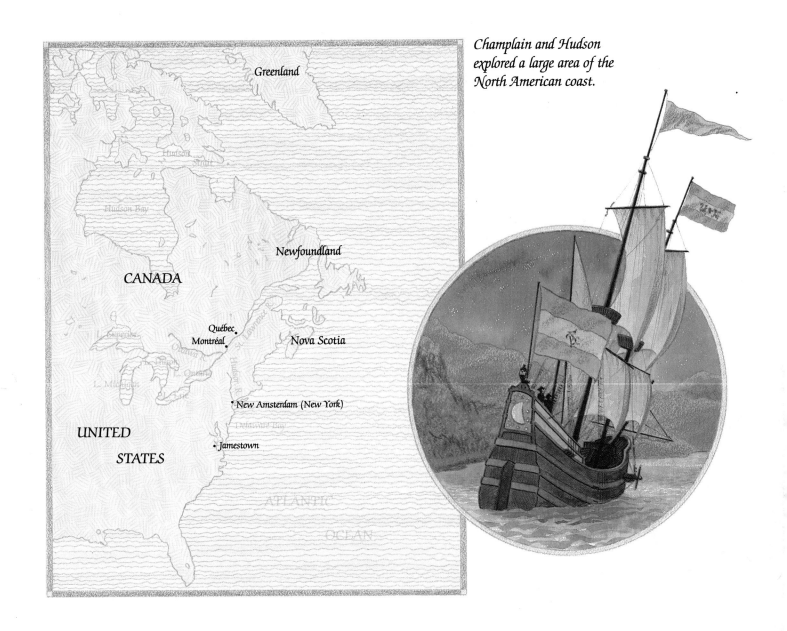

Champlain and Hudson explored a large area of the North American coast.

Greenland

CANADA

Newfoundland

Québec
Montréal

Nova Scotia

New Amsterdam (New York)

UNITED
STATES

Jamestown

ATLANTIC

OCEAN

The Dutch were also interested in North America, and in 1609 they sent Henry Hudson to search for a northern passage. His tiny ship, the *Half Moon*, with a crew of only twenty, sailed the coast from Maine to Virginia. They ventured north again, first to Delaware Bay and then up the big river that would later be named for Hudson. In 1611, on a second voyage, Hudson and his crew spent a terrible winter trapped in the icy waters of Hudson Bay. The crew mutinied and stranded Hudson and his young son, who were never seen or heard from again. Nevertheless, it was the voyages of Henry Hudson that led to the Dutch settlement of New York's Hudson Valley beginning in 1624.

The discovery of the Americas was of great importance to the countries of Europe. The search for a passage to the Far East was soon overshadowed by the quest for treasure—from rich deposits of precious metals to an abundant supply of furs, fish, and timber. In time, Europeans began to see the new land as something more: a future homeland for those seeking adventure, freedom, and fortune. The small early settlements would soon give way to a much larger migration of people to the New World. Europeans were drawn by the natural wealth and vast size of the Americas.

What was a boon to Europeans was a disaster for those who already
called the Americas home and for those brought here by force. In South
and Central America, native populations were nearly wiped out and the
survivors enslaved. In North America, white settlers pushed those they
called Indians westward, farther and farther from the places that had
been their homes. There would come a time when there would be no
place for them anywhere in America. The European settlers wanted all
of the land and its resources for themselves.

In the long saga of exploration in the New World, there were many failures. Most explorers never found what they were sent to find. Yet each voyage added to the growing picture of the size and shape of the new lands. The mapping of the Americas would take hundreds of years to complete, and in that time, new Americans from Europe, and later from other continents, would spread out to live everywhere in the New World. But the native cultures that existed in 1492 were either gone forever or reduced to mere fragments of the proud nations they once had been. The great gain of one people was the great loss of another.

Table of Dates

1492 First voyage of Christopher Columbus.

1494 Portugal and Spain sign the Treaty of Tordesillas, dividing the unexplored world between them.

1497–98 John Cabot makes two voyages to North America.

1498 The Portuguese reach India by sea.

1499 Amerigo Vespucci sails to South America.

1505 First African slaves brought to the Americas.

1507 The New World is named America after Amerigo Vespucci.

1513 Vasco Núñez de Balboa sights the Pacific Ocean.

1513–21 Juan Ponce de León explores in Florida.

1519–21 Destruction of the Aztec Empire in Mexico by the Spaniards. Hernán Cortés brings horses to the Americas.

1522 First documented voyage around the world, by Magellan's crew.

1523–24 The voyages of Giovanni da Verrazano.

1528–36 Alvar Núñez Cabeza de Vaca, with two other Spaniards and a Moroccan named Estevan, lives among native tribes in Texas.

1531–35 Francisco Pizarro in Peru. Inca civilization is destroyed by Spaniards.

1534–42 Jacques Cartier makes three voyages to Canada.

1539–42 Hernando de Soto explores in the southeast.

1540–42 Francisco Coronado leads a large expedition to search for gold. Small groups reach the Great Plains and California.

1562 John Hawkins brings African slaves to the West Indies.

1571–76 Martin Frobisher searches for a northwest passage.

1580 Francis Drake completes a voyage around the world.

1583 Humphrey Gilbert claims Newfoundland for England.

1585–87 John Davis makes three Arctic voyages attempting to locate a passage.

1585–87 Roanoke Island settled.

1588 The Spanish Armada is defeated by the English.

1603–15 Samuel de Champlain explores eastern Canada.

1607 Jamestown founded.

1609–11 The voyages of Henry Hudson.

1619 First legislative assembly in Virginia. Women and slaves arrive in Jamestown.

1620 Pilgrims land in Plymouth, Massachusetts.

1625 New Amsterdam settled by the Dutch.

Some Other Explorers

1500 *Pedro Álvares Cabral* explores and claims Brazil for Portugal.

1500–01 *Gaspar Corte-Real* sails to Labrador and Newfoundland for Portugal.

1523–34 *Pedro de Alvarado* with Cortés in Mexico. Explores and claims Guatemala for Spain.

1524 *Estevão Gomes* explores coast of New England and Nova Scotia for Spain.

1526 *Luis Vásquez de Ayllón* founds short-lived Spanish settlement along the Georgia coast.

1540 *García López de Cárdenas* with Coronado. Leads an expedition to the Grand Canyon.

1541–42 *Francisco de Orellana* travels the length of the Amazon River for Spain.

1542 *Juan Rodríguez Cabrillo* and *Bartolemé Ferrelo* explore the coast of California for Spain.

1562 *Jean Ribaut* sails along the Florida and South Carolina coast. Establishes a temporary French settlement in South Carolina.

1564–65 *René de Laudonnière* leads a French expedition to Florida coast. Settlers build Fort Caroline.

1565 *Pedro Menéndez de Avilés* arrives in Florida with a Spanish fleet. They kill French settlers and establish St. Augustine.

1566–67 *Juan Pardo* leads inland expedition along Savannah River. Explores areas of the southeast for Spain.

1585–86 *Richard Grenville* brings English colonists to Roanoke Island.

1586–88 *Thomas Cavendish* becomes the third person to sail around the world. Exploring for England, he travels along the west coast of South America, attacking Spanish towns.

1594–97 *Willem Barents,* a Dutch navigator, makes three voyages to search for a passage. First expedition to winter in the Arctic.

1598–1605 *Juan de Oñate* explores many areas of the southwest. Claims New Mexico for Spain.

1602–06 *Bartholomew Gosnold* sails along New England coast. Discovers Cape Cod and establishes trading post for England.

1605 *George Waymouth* explores coast of Maine and trades for furs for England.

1608–15 *Étienne Brulé* travels with Champlain. Lives among Hurons and is first explorer to reach the Great Lakes.

1612–16 *William Baffin* and *Robert Bylot* search for a northwest passage for England. They venture farther north than any other explorers before them. Their feat will not be surpassed for over 200 years.

1614 *Adriaen Block* explores Long Island Sound and the Connecticut River for the Dutch.

1615–16 *Willem Schouten,* a Dutch explorer, finds new route to the Pacific around Cape Horn.

North America 1500–1620

Before the coming of the Europeans, there were more than 1 million Native Americans living in North America. Some researchers believe that there may have been as many as 10 to 12 million. Warfare and disease took their toll on the native population, and by 1900, less than 250,000 Native Americans still lived in North America.

When the Europeans began to explore and claim parts of the continent for themselves, there were groups of Native Americans living in all areas of North America. Their lifeways were as varied as the regions they inhabited. Some were wanderers, or nomads; others lived in settlements both small and large. They were hunters and fishermen, farmers and builders, artisans, craftspeople, and inventors. They had rich religious and spiritual lives, sharing a deep kinship with the natural world. Some groups were peaceful and others warlike. They spoke hundreds of different languages, many of which are still spoken today.

The Europeans received many gifts from the native peoples. They were enriched by the interesting new foods, healing medicines, useful inventions, valuable natural resources, and wisdom and knowledge of the native peoples. The Europeans had much to offer as well, but instead of peaceful trading, they took what the native peoples had and offered little or nothing in return. They forced them off their lands, and by 1900, most surviving Native Americans were living on government reservations in misery and poverty. The legacy of the lives they once lived has yet to be appreciated and acknowledged.

Contacts Between Native Americans and European Explorers

NORTHEAST: Here are some of the tribes encountered by these explorers. In the northeast, many tribes belonged to Algonquian- or Iroquoian-speaking confederacies.

Brulé: Hurons, Susquehannocks

Cabot: Beothuks, Micmac, Abnaki, Massachusetts, Powhatans

Cartier: Beothuks, Micmac, Montagnais, Iroquois, Hurons

Champlain: Montagnais, Micmac, Ottawas, Hurons

Corte-Real: Beothuks, Micmac

Gosnold: Wampanoags

Hudson: Manhattans, Wappingers, Mahicans

Verrazano: Narragansett, Pokanoket, Abnaki, Penobscot, Catawba

SOUTHEAST:

De Soto: Timucuas, Seminoles, Tuskegees, Chickasaws, Choctaws, Creeks

Pardo: Cheraw

Ponce de León: Calusas, Timucuas

Ribaut: Timucuas, Cusabos, Saturiwas

SOUTHWEST:

Coronado (including other explorers who were part of this expedition): Zuni, Tiguex, Apache, Wichitas, Hopi, Pawnee, Mobiles, Napochis, Tahomes, Yuma, Cocopas, Mojaves, Halchidhomas, Hualapais

Oñate: Keres, Tiguex

OTHER CONTACTS:

Drake: Miwoks (Pacific coast)

Frobisher and Davis: Inuits (Arctic)

Jamestown: tribes of the Powhatan Confederacy

The Impact of the European Arrival in the Americas

In the years between 1500 and 1620, life in both North and South America was changed forever by the arrival of European explorers and settlers. The nature of the first contacts, the relationships between the native peoples and the Europeans, and the long-term results of these contacts were extremely varied. In South America, the Spaniards engaged in mining precious metals and operating plantations to grow the crops that would be profitable exports. With armies to enforce their will, they enslaved and killed much of the native population in the process.

Along the east coast of what is now the United States, the English came to settle and start new lives. Their disregard for the land rights of the inhabitants caused conflict and warfare, and the eventual displacement of these people. In Canada, the French developed complex trading relationships with a number of native tribes. They lived among them and learned their ways, but in the end, they too forced the native population to move inland or change their way of life. So, throughout the Americas, nothing remained the same. The European way of life gradually spread and the lifeways of the native peoples slowly disappeared.

Native American Contributions to the World

Here are some of the crops, products, and inventions of the peoples of the New World:

FOODS: avocados, beans, blueberries, cashews, cassavas, chocolate, cola drinks, corn, papayas, peanuts, pecans, peppers, pineapples, potatoes, pumpkins, squash, strawberries, sugar, sunflowers, tomatoes, vanilla, wild rice

OTHER PRODUCTS: asphalt, chewing gum, cotton, fabric dyes, rubber, sisal, tar, tobacco
MEDICINES: ipecac, petrolatum, quinine
INVENTIONS: canoes, dogsleds, hammocks, kayaks, moccasins, pipes, rubber balls, snowshoes, toboggans

American natives cultivated over three hundred food crops. They gave the world more than half of the crops that are cultivated today. The foods discovered in the Americas changed the diet and eating habits of people all over the world. Europeans also borrowed the advanced planting methods used by American natives, who made use of terracing, crop rotation, irrigation canals, and natural fertilizers such as fish meal and guano. The potato, in particular, was an important new addition to the European diet. There were many varieties and all were extremely nutritious. Potatoes could be easily grown and used in so many ways that they became a staple of the diet in many European countries.

European Colonies and Settlements in the New World

1502 Columbus founds first colony in the New World on Hispaniola.

1510 Port of Nombre de Dios founded by Spanish in Panama.

1515 City of Havana, Cuba, established by Spanish.

1521 Spanish found San Juan, Puerto Rico.

1526 Ayllón founds short-lived settlement of San Miguel de Gualdape in South Carolina.

1533 Cartagena, Colombia, founded as treasure city on Spanish Main.

1535 Lima, Peru, founded by Pizarro.

1536–37 Asunción, Paraguay, established by Spanish.

1537 New Spain established in Mexico.

1538 Bogotá, Colombia, founded by Spanish.

1541–43 Cartier founds a short-lived colony in Québec, Canada.

1545 Spanish start settlement at Potosí, Bolivia, to mine silver.

1554 Portuguese settle São Paulo, Brazil.

1562 Ribaut establishes French Charlesfort in South Carolina. Soon abandoned.

1564 French build Fort Caroline in Florida. Falls to Spanish, 1565.

1565 Menéndez founds St. Augustine, Florida. First permanent settlement in U.S.

1585 Roanoke Island settled.

1600 French found Tadoussac on St. Lawrence River.

1604 Sainte-Croix, in Canada, settled by French.

1605 French and English establish settlements in the West Indies.

1605 French found Port Royal, Nova Scotia.

1607 Jamestown founded.

1607 English build St. George Fort on Maine coast.

1608 Champlain founds Québec City.

1609 Oñate starts mission settlement at Santa Fe, New Mexico.

1610 English establish fishing colony at Cuperts Cove in Newfoundland.

1613–14 Dutch build Fort Nassau (Albany, New York).

1620 Pilgrims settle in Plymouth, Massachusetts.

1624–25 Dutch settle New Amsterdam (later New York City).

JUL   2001